Golden Dust

Poems

Charles Whittaker

OPEN ENDS PRESS

For Madeline K. Whittaker

CONTENTS

A Dancing Tree

Blake thought trees
Far off men,
Seen through the soul

Of sweet delight.
Since learning this,
I can't see a tree

Without thinking
Of Blake
And a little figure

Swaying in place
As he dances in tune
With the landscape.

Hymn to the Moon

First sight is beyond
Seeing, a beeline
Through the dark,

Blue
And white
Halo

Above ground,
Glimmering streaks
Alight in the dew.

First sight
In a bee's mind
Steers his flight,

And so, first sight
Calls to mind
A bee in flight

When my seeing
Steers me to you,
Honey-sweetened moon,

Sovereign of the Dew,
Sovereign of the Sky,
Restoring my mind

Through phases
And fermentations
In the night.

A Poet and His Book

How much I am
Like a book, waiting
For the eyes

That will bring me
Into being, that look,
That gleaming,

Murmuring love's
Shared
Secret meaning—

Oh, for the thrill
Of a finger running
Down my spine!

Song

Winding our way
Into death or into life, take
The fight out of life

And you will surely die,
As searching for a life
Of ease brings about

Disease, cankers
On the soul's endeavor.
I seek rather a concerted mind

And body, ripening together
In a clear autumnal light.
How we face death,

The near certain end,
Is how we will be
Remembered in life,

Ruby red and golden,
Fresh as morning,
Or dark as night.

Luna

Turning over, half awake,
Half asleep, I face the familiar
Enchantment of her whispering

On the pillow beside me, then
Seek to delineate her floating quietly
On waters within my mind—the air

Grows light—she is
Gone! —yet her image remains
An image of the Beyond.

In a Sunlit Room

If I'm sentimental,
It's to lost connections
I ultimately had

No connection to—
How strange!
Play on, heart, like

An old record,
Let memories fade like photos
In a sunlit room.

Strange how alike
The faces of my
Desired lovers were,

Dark hair, slight
Stature, with the eyes
Of my mother.

Play on, heart, she's gone.
If I'm sentimental,
I've forgotten the tune,

My record of broken love,
Memories
In a sunlit room.

Castaway

There's nothing to be gained
Through poetry except everything
Lost without it: love, dignity,

The world. The essence of
Tedium to those who died in
School, that it survives being

Scoffed at, reveals love, dignity,
And world in a new light,
A light itself formed,

Unformed, and reborn,
In a world where day and night
Revolve as one,

Where the poet gathers in stars
Word of his love
And the journey home.

In the Garden

Selfless ants,
Working in concert,
Overturn a leaf

In the garden
Just now, with,
I imagine, no

Thought
Of deity, just
Following

Their nature.
Between the ants
And I, who

Has more
Hope, who is
The wiser?

Or does God
Equally fulfill
All natures?

Spring

I admit I don't know
The purposes of time
Or existence, and so

Write letters that
Will never be
Received, hoping

That when spring arrives
In the flux
She may perhaps

Sigh without knowing
The reason why:
Life is tough.

All Thumbs

Prehistoric traces
Of whom I am
Found in the organism,

In the life of me,
Instincts of an animal
Who came before

Human eyes, with coded
Reflexes to a world
Neither within nor without,

Whose primal hands
Hold the object
Of the hunt,

A consciousness which,
Evolving, would give
Birth to divinity.

Though gods differ
In our beliefs, we share
Alike in thumbs.

Counting the Digits on My Hand

One has it
All, in
Potential.

Two, never
Alone, there's
Always two

Of everything—
Witness one's eyes,
Ears, hands & feet.

Three, between
You & I, an unstable
Elephant in the room.

Four, full circle,
With a start, one has
Been here before,

Without focus—oh,
The clear prescience of time
Turned inside out!

Five, quincunx,
The ultimate
Hand.

Pearls

1.

A perfect word
For shadow work—
Engrossing.

2.

Lacking an underworld,
You build a heaven
To your peril,

Peril,
The pearl
Of heaven.

3.

If God is dead,
He's found an afterlife
In my belief.

Musing on the Threshold of Hell

When I need to
Suffer, I don't decry
A lost paradise,

But go to hell,
For hell too is
Beautiful, in its

Place, in season,
Where lost
Souls are found,

Where the timeless
Depth of the grave
Through which I

Enter discloses
A presence uttering
In strange tongue,

A voice exciting
Sparks from darkness
And forging molten words,

Whose terrible rites
Of passage draw
Mind forth in sound—

Where I find joy, for here
Are no spirits
Who haven't suffered in clay.

Conversation in the Night

An envoy from the City of God
Appeared to me with this
Message in a dream: The brightest

In your world is but a shadow
Of light; forgetting
Your former home among

The stars, you leave a hole
In the Heart of Heaven,
While your love illuminates

A momentous depth in hell,
Above which you shudder
As rolling smoke parts,

Revealing rebirth in the rich
Black loam of the Nile.
My hell, I replied, constitutes

But another path to heaven,
Whose stars remain as
Beacons to my mind.

Criminal acts are committed
Under the void expression "God,"
While Osiris created order and unified

The land. Named, he speaks
To my heart. Besides, he's nearer
This world than heaven.

Noir

1.

A full moon projects its view
Through dark gulfs
In the clouds,

The trees shady characters
In the cinematic light,
Lone headlights

The roaming eyes
Of a cat
Returning home

From the prowl, as
Tomorrow's headline unrolls
Its dark conspiracy.

2.

He liked it when she wore
Sheer lingerie: it made him feel
He had X-ray vision.

When she mentioned
She was moving to another
City, he wondered

Whether telepathic powers
Lay in his latent inventory,
For something in her gripped him

From beyond. He likened it
To the ravishment of the Virgin.
To her it was only a job.

3.

Two late night strollers,
Voices mingling with the chimes,
Recede in silence.

4.

A lone phone booth
Lit on a lone road
At night—the night

Night hides from—
Where missing faces
Used to hang—

The faces gone now
Without a whisper,
The phone booth

No longer there.
I stepped in and am gone
Among the missing.

Lucifer and the Cat

1.

Our lives make
Not the difference
Our thoughts do,

As thought deals
With the excess
Of what we cannot

Realize in our lives.
A gray and white cat
Enters the room

And weaves her way
About my ankles,
In and out,

Rubbing her scent
Briskly
Against my legs.

My life as dear to me
As the cat's is
To her,

In this I imagine
All creatures
Are alike.

2.

The cat awakens
In shadows. Somewhere
In the desert

Sits an Archangel
With shrunken wings
And lewd glare

On a mountain
Of gold, monument
To a former age.

Cats came from
The desert. Many men
Have left their lives

In search of that gold,
Only to die
Of thirst in the heat,

From which the cat
Walked away untamed
Into the present day.

3.

A cat will not be taken
For anything less
Than itself.

Even Lucifer shrinks
From its independence,
His powerless wings

Receding in the air,
Though his hoard
Continue to allure.

It's not evil trying
To recapture some
Of the potential

Present in that gold.
Trouble comes
When one's thoughts

Turn rapacious,
Become subservient
To excess and never

Truly free, never able
To take hold
Of the gold.

4.

As this cat came
Through many bodies
To sit in my lap,

I too passed through
Many lives to sit
Beside her.

We don't think alike
Yet somehow
Our thought is the same,

Gold subsisting in us
Without a name,
Except love,

Our common nature,
In which tamed
And untamed unite

In morning star's light,
And I see in the cat
More than I can say.

Golden Rays

The sunlight so beautiful an opening
This morning, I had to step through it—
Inspired being, why do you lament?

To pet the cat this morning
Is a heavenly feeling: purr
After purr bounding away

To the horizon's peeping
On sinews folded beneath
His golden tabby fur.

Is it his purring beneath your fingers
Wakens a vision of the wild
Within your blood, a vibrant

Yearning, your lament
Far exceeding the beauty
Found in self-contentment?

Inspired being, why do you lament
With the sunlight so beautiful
An opening this morning?

A Fable of the Cat's Purring

I awaken to the cat speaking:
I sleep with one
Eye open and have

Nine lives, whereas
You're asleep
In the natural;

Murmur to me then
Of reason
Like a wild-eyed bee,

Who, in a quest
For nectar, fulfills
All he must do,

And so sweetens
A place
In the larger vale

For the next bee
To buzz by,
As truly as I speak.

The Prince of Darkness

Does evil serve
A purpose in making
Creation whole?

I venture out
On the narrowest
Of bridges

Into darkness
Without knowing
Whether my footing

Will bear weight,
Whether I indeed
Bear substance.

To fall on evil
Is to meet
The Prince

Of Darkness,
No less real
Than the Prince

Of Light, whom
We naturally
Adore.

Yet in truth one can
Only love a whole.
I must allow

The Prince of Darkness
Into my heart, a terrifying
Prospect, towards

Which I venture out
On a narrow bridge
Into darkness,

That I may face truth
Wholeheartedly
In body, mind and soul.

Rising Through the Roots of Life

It's a good thing
When a poet rises
From the dead

And greets you
With a challenge
And a smile.

It's difficult though
Bringing your life
Into accord:

It requires strength,
Patience
And critical insight,

But most of all
A sense of humor:
You think dead

They don't move,
But the dead think
Outside the boxes

They are buried in,
With a spirit that
Can't be contained.

Better a poet though
Than a devil
Looking for a soul.

The Flames

I rarefy what's hard
To find, or broaden it
For wider appeal,

Resisting the temptation
To cram everything
Into an understanding

Or cramp the reader's brain:
The sea travels far
On inland breezes.

I exaggerate like there's no
Tomorrow (there may not be),
And think somewhere,

In the innermost recess
Of desire, where flames
Are calm inhabitants

Of joy, lies the assembly
Whose decisions balance
The uncertainties of

The human heart,
Where awaits judgment.
I don't need to see more,

Only to know better
Of what I've seen,
My heart held

In the hands
Of the unseen, secure
In my belief.

Memory of the Sea

My body
A natural function

Of imagination,
With my ear

To a shell
I hear the sea

Where the sea
No longer is—

It is the same
With myself.

Self-Portrait

I am the face
Of many
Living together

We are my
Preferred
Pronoun

I remind us
We are not
All alike

Alive in the Everyday World

Each alike a blessing
And a curse, as vinegar
Hides sour and sweet:

To shun the sour
And demand all sweet
Leads to bitterness

And hollow mutters
Beneath the breath;
But sweet forgiveness

And the laying aside
Of grievances
Create a blessing

From a curse,
A legitimate hope
For an imperfect world.

And so, I approach
Strangers as I do vinegar:
Prepared to die.

Voices in Love

The learned fall in love
With the idea of love, with
The sound of their own

Voices. But if two meet
And share the same ideas,
Who can deny them

Their thoughts of love?
Perhaps theirs is the key
To an imperishable body,

Or an idea of it at least,
"The inner echo
Of words once spoken."

Golden Dust

The future
Is always being
Written.

The dead have
The advantage in that
Their voices

Are now in the heads
Of the living
As they flash before

Our eyes,
Their bodies
All soul now

Or golden dust,
Dying daily
To be reborn.

Cass

If I felt loved
For myself would I strive
So hard to recreate myself in poems?

When I followed my heart
Into perplexity
And entanglements,

You were always
There: "We've known
A lot of assholes,

But we hang
With the best," and other
Little words

Of encouragement
Mulled over
Morning coffee.

I read once
Of a marriage
After death,

I think in Jung,
And smile at the thought
Of death

As a renewal
Of your vows,
A perpetual anniversary,

As last night
You journeyed home
To Jack. Ah, Cass,

A consummate friend,
You were
Deserving of the best.

Shipley

His eyes were deep
Set coals, his beard,
White, as if swept

By tides. I knew him
As a cool fountainhead
Of knowledge,

Alive with a memory
Of time and place,
Surrounded by tropical lore.

He had a kindness,
A laugh that will be
Missed, as if Father Time

Himself stopped
And saw the humor
In it. Miami—

Miami lost a piece of
History today.
Rest in peace, John Shipley.

Eleanor

She's gone to the stars
Beyond tomorrow,
To be found

In the many lives
She touched: I know
I feel lighter

For sharing laughs
With her
Over some absurdity

In the world.
She was passionate
On women's rights,

Fair to all, and drew
Strength from an innate
Sense of justice.

I learned from her
How uncivilized
Male chauvinism

Can be, of those
Who will never relate
To a woman's psyche.

She may sound
Idealistic, but it is
Only as Athene

Tempered her mind.
A warm glow eases
My sadness tonight

On divining a Goddess
In the memory
Of my friend's life.

Musing

1.

Mind drifts into reminiscence
As old joys become
New pains,

While resistant seals,
Under flame, wax soft
And impressionable,

Yield to a humming repose
In the wine-cellar
Of my soul, where I muse,

Running my thumb
Along vintages housed
In that cryptic room.

2.

What is love
But a yearning
Felt rippling

Through the breast
For like yearnings
In other breasts,

The yearning itself
Immeasurable
In its oriental appearance

At time's awakening
Beyond reminiscence
And a renewal of seasons?

3.

I witness a strange déjà vu,
Having been here before
With none but myself,

Only to find another
In a time before myself,
Who chooses words

Carefully: Whoever was
Lost answering the call
Of the perpetual flame

Brooding within? In you
I see myself following
The Sun in so far as our

Natures can be known.
Darkened at times, lacking
Assurance, yet called on

To form a bright heart
And vision, we feel no loss
When life summons.

To reveal the timeless
Amid seasons
Is given to a few

For the benefit of
Many, done in the name
Of a celestial flame,

That his sacred image
May redeem our
Ignorance

And restore time
In person to a place
Called heaven.

Poem

1.

A host of what-ifs
And had-I-only-knowns
Clouding the air.

Had I only known
What I now know,
The before and after—

Doesn't matter:
Like bolts from the blue,
There's no assuaging,

Predicting, or predicating
Unexpected summons
From mystic origins,

Where one never knows
Unfolds as a basis
For thought.

2.

I passed through
A spell
Of bad poetry,

In which fear
Led me
To be selfish—

I couldn't give
Myself away.
Life, it's true, is

Easier lived
In the past, where
It can be in time

Forgotten, trying
To settle on
One.

3.

Clearly, my sight
Is off: I can't see
The things I am

Thinking of.
I shall never adjust to,
Nor tame,

The dark. So easy
To forget
What's before me,

Winding my way
Through interwoven
Serpentine paths

Of my own
Creation. Sun
Going down

Reminds me
Of a timeless
Order that sun

And self revolve
Around—in this
Sun and I are one.

Astonishment on Waking

The sun, half risen
From the cave mouth

Of hell, bright but
Inarticulate in itself

Escaping the dark,
Makes the physical fine

Lines of original light
And separates shadows

From leaves, revealing
The acacia tree outside

My window gleaming
Through dew like a vision

Wistfully imprinted
With the Tree of Life.

Post-It Note

49

A fucking nimbus—
And I must be at work
In an hour. Unforeseen

Contingencies
In the process
Of enlightenment

Remain to be
Worked out,
It seems.

Sunlit Dust in Air

God, a lovely way
Of saying, I'm
Not sure,

Invokes Blake's
Infinite
Hidden within,

Object of contemplation
In a garret
Of lone hours,

With cats, books,
A window looking out
Onto the street,

And motes of dust
Floating about
Streaming rays—

A lovely way
Of saying,
Bliss!

Naked

When I think of evolution
My mind goes back
To the turtle

And its primitive shield,
Alive today in a world
Artificial Intelligence is

Taking over. Poems
Following a design are more
Then a random array

Of words, though
The design never poke
Its head out

Or make itself known
Until long after
The artificer is gone.

There must be a reason
For this for one
Who does not see himself

As a poet. Is it
My clothes give me
Claustrophobia?

Reunion

I was wearing one of my father's
Old sweaters, when his voice laughed
From within—I am alive

As long as you wear that
Sweater. As surely as he baffled me,
I know now, being of one line,

What so baffled him: not knowing
What is needed. Forgiveness
Was much on my mind

As I offered him the life
He once took, realizing now
Why it was needed.

Longing

I long to hear the Father
At his Word, in Spirit, not in laws
That turn me away: is He

Likewise forever perplexed
As to what comes next?
Is complexity His

Natural language?
Who is His Beloved?
In ignorance is tyranny.

May the Father come to me
In words I can embrace,
May His form perfect my longing.

Notes from the Interview

Everything goes well
With CBD. As
High precepts of Art

Suggest an endless
Fascination
In the Eyes of God,

Nothing is lost on Him.
God and man
Go hand in hand:

The art He inspires
Alone survives.
He is inmost

To the outermost
Man, and breathes
Through us on earth.

Gentle, His fury
Can be that
Of a devil:

We are His comfort
And His curse,
We destroyed a planet.

Afternoon Musings

On a projected
Reality—the sensible—
I can't take credit for—

What makes it so
Funny—what fictitious power
Dreamt it up,

As in a time without
Beginning or end? As I am
Sensible, I wonder

About my place
In it, how subject to death,
I know nothing but panic

At a loss of the literal,
Yet preserving something
Of the dreamer within.

Evening Rapture

A little puff
And the night turns blue.

A sprinkle
And stars sparkle

In the sky.
The hand of the Lord

Is matter's
Make believe power.

Walls

I've learned transparency
Is the only thing
That allows me to pass

Through walls. I began
In my body, where I
Encountered the roots

Of mind and soul,
Wholly endeavoring
To be honest—but

What's that?   I know
Deep down
I am a fiction, who is

Nevertheless real. I know
The world throws up
Walls. The secret

To the walls is they are
Invented, made up
In mind's eye,

So that their substance
Is not solid but fictive
To the desiring soul.

Walls are the world's way
Of saying get over it
To a soul passing through.

Alive in the Moment

59

When asked about death,
Confucius replied, You ask about
Death when you haven't yet

Learned how to live.
To know the beginning
Is to know the end.

It's better to feel you're going
To live forever than to forever think
You're going to die.

Elegy

for Jamie Humet

1.

The guilt I feel
Forgetting the dead

Until even guilt
Is forgotten. One day

I too will die
And life go on.

That life goes on
Is a form of western will—

I will be forgotten
Against my will.

2.

Ah, Jamie, murdered
In your car outside an ATM

Monday night,
The timeless verities

Of who, where, why,
Resolved for you,

Remain hidden from me:
I slowly grasp you're gone

And, stunned,
Ask, Who? Why?

3.

As grief is heard
Among the living

Recalling the dead
As they were in life,

Now lost to life,
You still hold value

In this world. Let me
Add my voice: there's

No closure in death
Other than that life goes on,

Albeit without you,
Without me;

Mortal, then, we pass
Through life's immortality.

Ah, Jamie, may you breathe
In these words

Amidst the verities
In a grove of peace.

Amazing Grace

1.

Church puts death in a place
I don't want to go.

Better this great white egret
Landing on the lawn

Outside my window—
A phenomenon

Never seen before—at 11 a.m.,
The hour of your service.

2.

Soul and nature
Need somehow

Coincide. Soul
Is Nature

In man. Bird
Is Soul

In flight. This bird
Landed.

3.

I guess, Jamie,
You're here

To stay, or
To say

You've gone away
For good.

The egret's
Color says,

Either way,
It's good,

For white contains
All shades.

4.

The mourners,
I imagine, are dressed

In black;
I sit writing this

In pajamas, paying
My respects.

I want to be at home
With death: had I been

In the cathedral,
I would have missed the bird

And Jamie's soul
Landing outside the window.

An Infant Soul

May you smile when fortune smiles,
Feel balance and composure
Under threatening skies.

May you learn to walk
With coordination and precision
Out of a trap at any time.

I watch you toddling about
Your mother's lap and wonder
What future will make a memory

Of your soul, or whether you
Will pass a prophet on the road
Who reveals you in a glimpse

Beside yourself, lone witness
To your soul's rebirth. Patience yet,
In you, time itself is undecided.

My Heart Goes Out

In an escape so small my eye
Was drawn near to it by chance,
The bird, sprung by whatever

Twist in the fabric of the elderly
Woman's life threw open
The hinges of the cage that day,

Disappeared twittering from view;
And later the poor soul wandering
The neighborhood, looking up

Into trees for her lost little budgie.
I witnessed a small death
In another that day, felt her loss,

My being gone into hers while hers
Came into mine, so that we were
Forever stitched together

In the wild world of mischance,
Where accidents happen
In a design so remote

As to be hidden from the eye,
Only to alight tragically in the fabric
Woven through our lives.

Evening News

People going over the edge
Taking selfies—I don't know
Whether to laugh or to cry.

A woman from West Virginia
Fell five floors
From a rooftop in NY.

She was a long way from home.
Falling was probably
The last thing on her mind.

A witness reported
A massive crash.
Luckily, she survived

With a fractured pelvis
And miscellaneous broken bones.
Amidst this tragedy,

A photo of a smiling,
Attractive woman. What is it
About panoramas

And a loss of self-awareness,
Universals
And the loss of common sense?

Sinead

Damn the gross
And corrupt,
Damn them all:

As if your own demons
Weren't enough,
They demonized you,

As they do to all
With outspoken views.
But how the register

Of your voice soars
High tonight
Above the pain!

I will hold a moment
Of silence for you
In 7 hours & 15 days,

Simply to thank you
For that song,
Its heartfelt refrain.

Trickster

I guess I use "is" a lot
Because I can't do a thing
Without existence—

But, damn it, someone stole
My shoes again
In a dream last night,

Brown shoes
My father
Gave me.

Obviously, I must walk
The paths barefoot
Without him.

The Biosphere

1.

Autumnal blue
Skies in Miami are
As natural as breathing,

With the occasional
Cloud a sneeze
Brought on by allergens.

As above,
So below—
But between?

I'm going out of my mind
Trying to find a place
In my mind,

A human creature
Spanning
Earth and heaven.

2.

We're seeking
To create in machines
What nature

Woke in us—
Does something
Beyond us

Will this?
I don't know.
If we want to live

Forever, we
Will have to struggle
To incorporate

Alien technologies
Within our craft,
The biosphere dying.

While the aeon turns,
Machines may think,
But we'll still feel pain.

Gaia

73

Soon the oceans
Will be plastic,

The forests bare.
So why complain

If I'm losing my hair?
It's human nature,

Uncontrollable,
Unlike industrial waste.

As in a Crystal Ball

With AI chips in our brains,
We'll drone on forever, especially
If our natural organs

Have been replaced
By synthetic variants.
Of course, we will be programmed

To thrive in warmer
Climes, and war
Will truly be insane.

I hope this is a brain blurb,
Not a premonition, as we will grow
Nostalgic for death.

Canvassing the Universe

There's a lot
Of pre-recorded
Messages

In space. No one
Answers. Maybe that's
A good thing.

Man thinks highly
Of himself. Perhaps
We've been quarantined.

Why I'll Never Be President

If he wins re-election
When they can't manage
A pandemic,

What will they do
When the aliens arrive?
Just for kicks,

If I were the challenger,
I'd insert that
Into a debate,

Then with _a_ serious look,
Turn and wink
Into the camera!

The Critic

The possibility
Of quarantine offers
A reason why

Toilet paper is
Disappearing
From the shelves—

People rear-ended
By the plague,
He thought,

As an afterthought,
Already gone
From the scene:

He had plenty
Of books at
Home.

Blake

You need to walk
Down many streets
Before being able

To say it's not a song
In the streets,
The world is not so

Easily let go of
With its Babylonian
Festivals.

But the quiet,
Calm and persistent
Calling

To reopen Blake—
How sweet and alive
That song.

A Common Tongue

Approaching life
Through a lens
Of poetry as best

I can, I've learned
If it's only to be
Seen through that

With which I agree,
Then I've lost
The complete picture,

Life striking me
As an intense
Focus throughout,

With impulses forming
The self-evident
Organisms

Passing through the mind's eye.
A common tongue may have
Been spoken once,

Essence of the word
Universal. I hear it keenly
In words, I comprehend

Yet disagree with,
While failing to comprehend
My own response.

It remains in the words
Hearts long to hear,
Joined by instinct

To desire. Once
This tongue was the focus
Of a complete life;

Now, I'm struck dumb
With disbelief, as if,
In essence, I stand selfless,

Reflecting on God's nature
Within myself
And other creatures,

While one with Creation.

Honeybee

Truth only hurts
When resisted—

Be your own
Golden Reader,

Accepting of
Your contrary,

And no criticism
Can sting.

What doesn't apply,
Cast aside—

In your own words,
Your own words.

The Afflatus

1.

I want to live
In the world

Without being
A world figure:

I am as I am,
A voice in the wind.

Only concerned
Inescapably

With how others
Think of me,

My great gift,
Given freely—

Surprise! —
Is wrapped

In paranoia:
Voices in the wind.

2.

I would be happy
If my heart was in

The right place.
I am unhappy

My heart is so
Out of place.

I feel the breeze
On my face,

The breeze is never
Out of place.

I mean well, but
Like the wind, beholden

To myself alone,
I am an evildoer

To myself
And to my friends.

3.

The afflatus is
Divine, conceit,

Natural; for every
Divine thought

There is a natural
Conceit then,

In which the voices
Play a part, as driven

On the wind, they are
Free of opinion.

Heaven

Ok, so I sniff
Women's perfumes
As they pass by,

But does that mean
I should then walk
Off a cliff?

The desire
To see through,
And not with,

The eye is
The surest step
To a vertical ascent.

Strange

How strange, I fell
In love
With a nose—

I didn't know it
At the time,
But that to me

Was all eternity—
A nose!
How very strange.

In the Children's Room at the Library

Little fart, untamed
Wind, you will never find
A friend, your fate,

To fill the room
With disgust: parents
Will disown you,

Strangers will turn
Their noses up in abhorrence
As you pass,

Little urchin that you are—
Only one watches this scene
And secretly laughs.

It's a Wonderful Life

1.

Whenever I get a sudden taste
And a craving for wings,

I know somewhere in Buffalo
An angel has gotten his wings.

2.

Whereas Wheaties pose

As the Breakfast of Champions,

Ramen Instant Noodles
Are the stuff of survivors—

Nom, nom, nom,
A warm, hearty broth

To fill the cold
Vacancies of a soul.

Joy

1.

I've been dinged
A couple of times
In life—that's life.

I'm only waiting
For the dong—
What joy to become

A complete
Ding dong—
A thought.

2.

I may be a detestable man,
To attest that misery is the utter lack

Of joy. But how is it then
That joy is never lost

On misery? What joy in an agony
Of unfathomable beauty!

3.

How can I be so certain,
Relying often
On the affirmative word

Is? Beware
The evangelical,
He'll rip your heart out, Jim.

I'll never accept terms
And conditions
For joy.

4.

Joy is very
Close to you,

Seen backwards
In a mirror—

What joy
If I were

That close
To you!

5.

If I bring you joy,
I bring myself joy,
A resounding bliss,

And alone on
A night like this,
Twice the happiness.

The Egret

Motionless white bird
Reflected in air, water—
Doubles on a branch.